WOLFGANG AMADEUS MOZART

SYMPHONY No. 29

A major/A-Dur/La majeur

Edited by
Richard Clarke

T0081280

Ernst Eulenburg Ltd

London · Mainz · Madrid · New York · Paris · Prague · Tokyo · Toronto · Zürich

CONTENTS

The present edition of Mozart's Symphony No.29 K201 is based on readings of
the relevant texts published in *Wolfgang Amadeus Mozart: Neue Ausgabe
sämtlicher Werke*, IV/11.5

PREFACE

The two major landmarks on Mozart's path to first maturity as a symphonist are generally held to be the 'Little' G minor Symphony, K183 (1773), and the Symphony in A major, K201 (1774). Indeed it is hard to find a single dissenting voice on this point. For Stanley Sadie, K183 and K201 mark Mozart's 'emergence from a preternaturally gifted youth into a great composer.'[1] Concert audiences would appear to agree: for the best part of a century they have consistently been the earliest of Mozart's symphonies to maintain a place in the standard orchestral repertoire. K201 has long been a special favourite with commentators. Alfred Einstein singled it out as one of 'Mozart's finest creations', and praised the first movement's central development section as 'the richest and most dramatic Mozart had written up to this time'.[2] Hans Keller found in it 'an unprecedented and, at this stage, unsuspected degree of profundity', and pronounced the first movement's opening theme as 'one of Mozart's greatest discoveries'.[3] More recently Neal Zaslaw has noted its 'thoroughgoing excellence'.[4] Whatever Mozart himself might have made of such remarks, he certainly thought well enough of the symphony to request his father to send the music on to him – along with the neighbouring symphonies K182, K183 and K204 – 'as quickly as possible'[5] two years after his permanent move to Vienna in 1781.

How had Mozart arrived at this new freedom and mastery? No doubt his recent visit to Vienna with his father, Leopold, had been a major stimulus, even though their hopes (expressed cryptically in some of Leopold's letters) of finding a post at the Imperial Court had come to nothing. The Mozarts returned to their Salzburg home on 27 September 1773. Just over a week later Mozart had completed the G minor Symphony K183; K201 was finished on 6 April the following year. However, Mozart would have found little encouragement for this new adventurousness from his employer. The Archbishop of Salzburg, Count Hieronymus Colloredo, was a cultured man, inclined towards reform within the church, and up to a point sympathetic to the more widely-shared views of the 18th-century 'Enlightenment'; but – in common with many aristocrats of the time – he regarded musicians as servants, and seems to have taken little, if any pride in the young Mozart's growing international reputation. The Archbishop saw two functions for music: either as entertainment (serenatas, divertimentos or suitably lightweight concertos) or for church services – in which case the music should be as condensed and unostentatious as possible.

Mozart's increasing frustration with the Archbishop's attitudes and behaviour towards him is well documented. Given all this, it is unlikely that he summoned up his full mastery in K201 to please his current employer. Possibly he was hoping for an attention-grabbing success somewhere else. The above-quoted letter to Leopold Mozart suggests that he still thought it might perform that useful function nine years later in Vienna. Still, K201 does not begin with a conventional call to attention. The opening theme is presented *piano*, with exploratory harmonies in the lower strings. The theme's full *forte* blossoming, with elegant imitative counterpoint in the bass, is held back until bar 13. This is in marked contrast to the driving syncopated unison theme that sets the first movement of K183 in motion. While the

[1] *The New Grove Dictionary of Music and Musicians*, ed. Stanley Sadie (London, 1980), 12, 690
[2] Alfred Einstein, *Mozart: His Character, His Work* (New York, 1945; repr. 1965)
[3] *The Symphony, Vol I: Haydn to Dvořák*, ed. Robert Simpson (Harmondsworth, 1966), 66–7
[4] Neal Zaslaw, *The Compleat Mozart: A Guide to the Musical Works of Wolfgang Amadeus Mozart* (New York, 1990), 193
[5] Letter to Mozart's father, Vienna, 4 January 1783

'Little' G minor Symphony can be seen as a brilliant youthful response to the so-called 'Sturm und Drang' ('storm and stress' or 'yearning') style typified by Haydn's Symphony No. 39 (also in G minor), K201 is altogether subtler. True, the intense string tremolandos in bb19–22 of the first movement and the dramatic *piano-forte* alternations that follow are classic 'Sturm und Drang' features, which can again be observed throughout the finale. However, the symphony also shows the influence of Haydn's symphonic wit: especially in the repeated-note oboe-horn fanfares in the Menuetto, whose meaning seems to shift teasingly according to its context (most strikingly when the full strings take it up, *fortissimo*, in b12), and in the rapid upward scale for violins in the finale (first heard in bb60–61). On one level the appearances of the latter are, in Neal Zaslaw's words, 'clear aural signposts to articulate the movement's formal structure'. At the same time there is something slightly disconcerting about the gesture: for a moment one may find oneself wondering exactly where the 'clear aural signpost' is pointing.

The *Andante* on the other hand is eloquent and sensuous, with the violins muted throughout (until the final *forte* statement in the Coda). The melodic style again recalls Haydn in places, but Mozart shows his hand in the richer inner voices: for example in bb9–13, where Haydn would probably have opted for something leaner and more transparent. The arresting high *forte* interjections in bb62 and 64, and the subsequent wide leaps in the melodic line are also much more characteristic of Mozart. Hearing such moments – and still more when one views the symphony as a whole – it is sobering to remember that this fresh, confident and sophisticated work is the product of an 18-year-old mind.

Stephen Johnson

VORWORT

Die „kleine" g-Moll-Sinfonie, KV 183 (1773), und die Sinfonie in A-Dur, KV 201 (1774), gelten gewöhnlich als die beiden größten Meilensteine auf Mozarts Weg zur ersten Reife als Sinfoniker. Man findet in der Tat kaum eine einzige abweichende Meinung bezüglich dieses Punktes. Für Stanley Sadie markieren die Sinfonien KV 183 und KV 201 Mozarts „Übergang von einem außergewöhnlich begabten Jugendlichen zu einem hervorragenden Komponisten."[1] Das Konzertpublikum scheint dieser Ansicht zuzustimmen: Die frühen Sinfonien Mozarts sind seit fast einem Jahrhundert ein fester Bestandteil des Standardrepertoires für Orchester. Die Sinfonie KV 201 war lange Zeit bei den Kommentatoren sehr beliebt. Alfred Einstein bezeichnete sie als „eine von Mozarts besten Schöpfungen" und lobte den zentralen Durchführungsteil des ersten Satzes als „das Reichste und Dramatischste, was Mozart bis zu diesem Zeitpunkt geschrieben hat."[2] Hans Keller findet in dem Werk „einen beispiellosen und in diesem Stadium unerwarteten Grad an Tiefgründigkeit" und bezeichnet das Eröffnungsthema des ersten Satzes als „eine von Mozarts größten Entdeckungen".[3] Erst unlängst stellte Neal Zaslaw die „grundlegende Qualität"[4] des Werkes heraus. Was auch immer Mozart selbst zu solchen Anmerkungen gesagt hätte, so fand er die Sinfonie immerhin so gut, dass er seinen Vater zwei Jahre nach seinem endgültigen Umzug nach Wien im Jahre 1781 darum bat, ihm die Komposition – zusammen mit den benachbarten Sinfonien KV 182, KV 183 und KV 204 – „so schnell wie möglich"[5] nachzuschicken.

Wie hat Mozart diese neue Freiheit und Meisterschaft erlangt? Der jüngste Besuch in Wien mit seinem Vater Leopold war zweifellos eine der Hauptanregungen, auch wenn die Hoffnungen (die in einigen von Leopolds Briefen etwas versteckt ausgesprochen wurden), eine Stelle am kaiserlichen Hof zu erhalten, enttäuscht wurden. Die Mozarts kehrten am 27. September 1773 nach Salzburg zurück. Nur eine Woche später hatte Mozart die Sinfonie in g-Moll, KV 183, vollendet; die Sinfonie KV 201 wurde am 6. April des folgenden Jahres fertig gestellt. Allerdings wird Mozart für diese neue Abenteuerlust wenig Zuspruch von seinem Arbeitgeber erhalten haben. Der Erzbischof von Salzburg, Graf Hieronymus Colloredo, war ein kultivierter Mann, der zu einer Reform innerhalb der Kirche tendierte und bis zu einem gewissen Punkt Sympathien für die weit verbreiteten Ansichten der „Aufklärung" des 18. Jahrhunderts hegte. Aber er betrachtete – wie auch viele der Aristokraten zu jener Zeit – Musiker als Diener und schien wenig oder keinen Stolz für die zunehmende internationale Reputation Mozarts empfunden zu haben. Der Erzbischof sah zwei Funktionen in der Musik: Sie diente entweder der Unterhaltung (Serenaden, Divertimenti oder geeignete leichte Konzerte) oder für Gottesdienste, wobei die Musik hierfür so komprimiert und schlicht wie möglich sein sollte.

Mozarts zunehmende Frustration bezüglich der Haltung und des Verhaltens des Erzbischofs ihm gegenüber ist gut dokumentiert. Angesichts all dieser Tatsachen ist es unwahrscheinlich, dass er sein gesamtes Können für die Komposition der Sinfonie KV 201 aufgebracht hat, um seinem damaligen Arbeitgeber zu gefallen. Möglicherweise hoffte er, anderswo mit einer erfolgreichen Aufführung auf sich aufmerksam machen zu können. Der oben zitierte Brief an Leopold Mozart deutet an, dass er noch immer der Meinung war, das Werk könne neun Jahre

[1] *The New Grove Dictionary of Music and Musicians*, hrsg. von Stanley Sadie (London, 1980), Band 12, S. 690.
[2] Alfred Einstein: *Mozart: His Character, His Work* (New York, 1945), Neuauflage 1965.
[3] *The Symphony, Vol I: Haydn to Dvořák*, hrsg. v. Robert Simpson (Harmondsworth, 1966), S. 66–67.
[4] Neal Zaslaw: *The Compleat Mozart: A Guide to the Musical Works of Wolfgang Amadeus Mozart* (New York, 1990), S. 193.
[5] Brief an Mozarts Vater, Wien, 4. Januar 1783.

später in Wien diese nützliche Funktion erfüllen. Trotzdem zieht die Sinfonie KV 201 zu Beginn nicht, wie sonst oft üblich, alle Aufmerksamkeit auf sich. Das Eröffnungsthema wird vielmehr im Piano vorgestellt, und die Harmonien in den tiefen Streichern gehen auf Entdeckungsreise. Erst in Takt 13 blüht das Thema dann im Forte mit einem eleganten nachahmenden Kontrapunkt im Bass vollständig auf. Dies steht in scharfem Gegensatz zu dem treibenden synkopischen Thema, das den ersten Satz der Sinfonie KV 183 charakterisiert. Während die „kleine" g-Moll-Sinfonie als hervorragende jugendliche Antwort auf den so genannten Stil des „Sturm und Drang" angesehen werden kann, der durch Haydns Sinfonie Nr. 39 (ebenfalls in g-Moll) geschaffen wurde, so ist die Sinfonie KV 201 doch insgesamt subtiler. Die intensiven Tremolos in den Streichern (Takt 19–22) im ersten Satz und die folgenden dramatischen Piano-Forte-Wechsel sind klassische Sturm-und-Drang-Merkmale, die man noch einmal im gesamten Finale finden kann. Die Sinfonie weist jedoch auch Einflüsse von Haydns sinfonischem Stil auf: Dies wird besonders deutlich im Menuett bei den sich wiederholenden Oboen-Horn-Fanfaren, deren Bedeutung sich dem Kontext entsprechend spielerisch zu verlagern scheint (besonders auffallend, wenn die vollen Streicher dies in Takt 12 im Fortissimo aufnehmen) sowie im Finale bei den schnellen aufsteigenden Tonleitern in den Violinen (erstmals in den Takten 60–61 zu hören). Letztere sind in Neal Zaslaws Worten „deutliche akustische Wegweiser, die die formale Struktur des Satzes ausdrücken". Gleichzeitig hat dieser Gestus auch einen etwas beunruhigenden Aspekt, da man sich möglicherweise im ersten Moment fragt, in welche Richtung der „deutliche akustische Wegweiser" zeigt.

Das Andante hingegen ist eloquent und sinnlich, die Violinen haben durchweg Pause (bis zum Schlussteil in der Coda). Der melodische Stil erinnert stellenweise wieder an Haydn, aber Mozart konzentriert sich auf die reichen Mittelstimmen, z. B. in den Takten 9–13; hier hätte Haydn wahrscheinlich einen etwas schlankeren und transparenteren Kompositionsstil gewählt. Die eindrucksvollen hohen Zwischenrufe im Forte in den Takten 62 und 64 sowie die darauf folgenden weiten Sprünge in der Melodielinie sind ebenfalls sehr charakteristisch für Mozart. Wenn man solche Momente hört – und noch mehr, wenn man die Sinfonie als Ganzes betrachtet – erinnert man sich mit Ernüchterung daran, dass dieses frische, überzeugende und anspruchsvolle Werk das Produkt eines erst 18-Jährigen ist.

Stephen Johnson
Übersetzung: Uta Pastowski

PRÉFACE

La «petite» Symphonie en *sol* mineur, K.183 (1773) et la Symphonie en *la* majeur, K.201 (1774) sont généralement, et sans voix discordantes sur ce point, citées comme les deux principales étapes jalonnant le cheminement de Mozart vers sa maturité de symphoniste. Pour Stanley Sadie, les K.183 et K.201 marquent chez Mozart : « l'émergence d'un grand compositeur chez un jeune homme surnaturellement doué ».[1] Le public de concert semble s'être rattaché à cet avis car, depuis près d'un siècle, ces œuvres ont régulièrement été les plus anciennes symphonies de Mozart à figurer en bonne place dans le répertoire orchestral courant. La Symphonie K.201 a constitué un sujet d'analyse favori des commentateurs. Alfred Einstein y vit l'une «des plus belles créations de Mozart» et décrivit le développement central de son premier mouvement comme « le plus riche et le plus dramatique écrit par Mozart jusqu'à cette époque. »[2] Hans Keller y trouva « un degré de profondeur sans précédent et inattendu à ce stade », et déclara le thème initial du premier mouvement « l'une des plus grandes inventions de Mozart. »[3] Plus récemment, Neal Zaslaw releva son « excellence permanente ».[4] Quelle qu'aurait été la réaction de Mozart à ces commentaires, il pensait, à l'évidence, assez de bien de cette symphonie pour demander à son père de lui en envoyer la partition – en même temps que celles des symphonies K.182, K.183 et K.204 de la même période – « aussi vite que possible »[5] deux ans après s'être définitivement installé à Vienne en 1781.

Comment Mozart était-il parvenu à cette liberté et à cette maîtrise nouvelles ? Il ne fait pas de doute que sa récente visite à Vienne en compagnie de son père, Leopold, constitua pour lui un important stimulant, bien que leurs espoirs (exprimés à demimots dans certaines lettres de Leopold) de lui trouver une situation à la cour impériale n'eussent pas abouti.

Les Mozart père et fils regagnèrent Salzbourg le 27 septembre 1773. Environ une semaine plus tard, Mozart avait achevé la Symphonie en *sol* mineur, K.183. La Symphonie K.201 fut terminée le 6 avril de l'année suivante. Toutefois, Mozart ne reçut que peu d'encouragements à se lancer dans cette nouvelle aventure de la part de son employeur. L'archevêque de Salzbourg, le comte Colloredo, homme cultivé, intéressé par la réforme de l'Eglise et, jusqu'à un certain point, partisan de l'esprit largement diffusé des «Lumières» du XVIIIème siècle, considérait néanmoins – comme beaucoup d'aristocrates de son temps – les musiciens comme des serviteurs et ne semble pas avoir montré la moindre fierté face à la réputation internationale grandissante du jeune Mozart. L'archevêque reconnaissait deux fonctions à la musique : le divertissement (sérénades, divertissements ou concertos légers) ou le service sacré, pour lequel la musique se devait d'être aussi concise que possible et dénuée de toute ostentation.

La frustration croissante ressentie par Mozart devant l'attitude et les comportements de l'archevêque à son égard est bien connue et il est peu probable, dans ces circonstances, qu'il ait déployé toute sa maîtrise dans la Symphonie K.201 pour plaire à son employeur. Sans doute espérait-il que son succès attirerait l'attention sur lui ailleurs. Sa lettre à Leopold Mozart citée ci-dessus semble indiquer que, neuf ans plus tard, il estimait toujours la Symphonie K.201 digne de servir cet objectif à Vienne. Toutefois, celle-ci ne débute pas par un épisode particulièrement fracassant au sens conventionnel. Son thème initial, présenté dans la nuance *piano* et comportant des harmonies complexes

[1] *The New Grove Dictionary of Music and Musicians*, Vol. XII, éd. Stanley Sadie, Londres, 1980, p.690
[2] Alfred Einstein, *Mozart: His Character, His Work*, New York, 1945, réimpr. 1965
[3] *The Symphony*, éd. Robert Simpson, Vol. I : *Haydn to Dvořák*, Harmondsworth, 1966, pp.66–67
[4] Neal Zaslaw, *The Complete Mozart : A Guide to the Musical Works of Wolfgang Amadeus Mozart*, New York, 1990, p.193
[5] Lettre de Mozart à son père, Vienne, 4 janvier 1783

des cordes graves, dont l'épanouissement complet, dans la nuance *forte*, et l'élégant contrepoint en imitation à la basse sont retardés jusqu'à la mesure 13, constitue un contraste marqué avec l'engageant thème à l'unisson syncopé qui amorce le premier mouvement de la « petite » Symphonie K.183 en *sol* mineur. Tandis que cette dernière se présente comme une réponse brillante et pleine de jeunesse au mouvement du « *Sturm und Drang* » (« *Orage et passion* ») incarné par la Symphonie n⁰ 39 de Haydn (également en *sol* mineur), la Symphonie K.201 se révèle plus subtile. S'il est vrai que les *tremolando* intenses des cordes des mesures 19 à 22 du premier mouvement et les alternances dramatiques de *piano* et *forte* qui suivent sont d'authentiques traits *Sturm und Drang* également rencontrés dans tout le *finale*, la symphonie témoigne, néanmoins, de l'influence de l'esprit humoristique des symphonies de Haydn, notamment par les fanfares des hautbois et des cors en notes répétées du *Menuetto*, dont la signification apparaît comme une facétieuse digression dans son contexte (en particulier au retour *fortissimo* de toutes les cordes, à la mesure 12), et par la gamme ascendante rapide des violons dans le *finale* (apparue en premier lieu dans les mesure 60–61). Dans une certaine mesure, ces éléments constituent, selon les termes de Neal Zaslaw : « de claires indications sonores qui articulent la structure formelle du mouvement ». Dans le même temps, il y a quelque chose de déconcertant dans leur intervention : on peut un instant se demander la direction montrée par « la claire indication sonore ».

L'*Andante*, à l'inverse, est éloquent et sensuel, les violons y utilisant la sourdine d'un bout à l'autre. Le style mélodique évoque de nouveau celui de Haydn à certains endroits, mais Mozart y déploie ses qualités propres dans les riches voix internes, ainsi, par exemple, dans les mesures 9 à 13, où Haydn aurait sans doute choisi moins de densité et plus de transparence. Les saisissantes ponctuations *forte* des mesures 62 et 64, ainsi que les larges intervalles mélodiques qui les complètent sont également beaucoup plus caractéristiques du style de Mozart. Il reste déconcertant, à l'écoute de tels moments – et, qui plus est, de la symphonie dans son intégralité – se rappeler que cette œuvre fraîche, confiante et sophistiquée est due à un jeune esprit de dix-huit ans.

Stephen Johnson
Traduction : Agnès Ausseur

SYMPHONY No. 29

Wolfgang Amadeus Mozart
(1756–1791)
K 201

I. Allegro moderato

Edited by Richard Clarke
© 2010 Ernst Eulenburg Ltd, London
and Ernst Eulenburg & Co GmbH, Mainz

2

11

12

14

18

Coda

III. Menuetto

Trio

Menuetto da capo

IV. Allegro con spirito

26

28

30

32